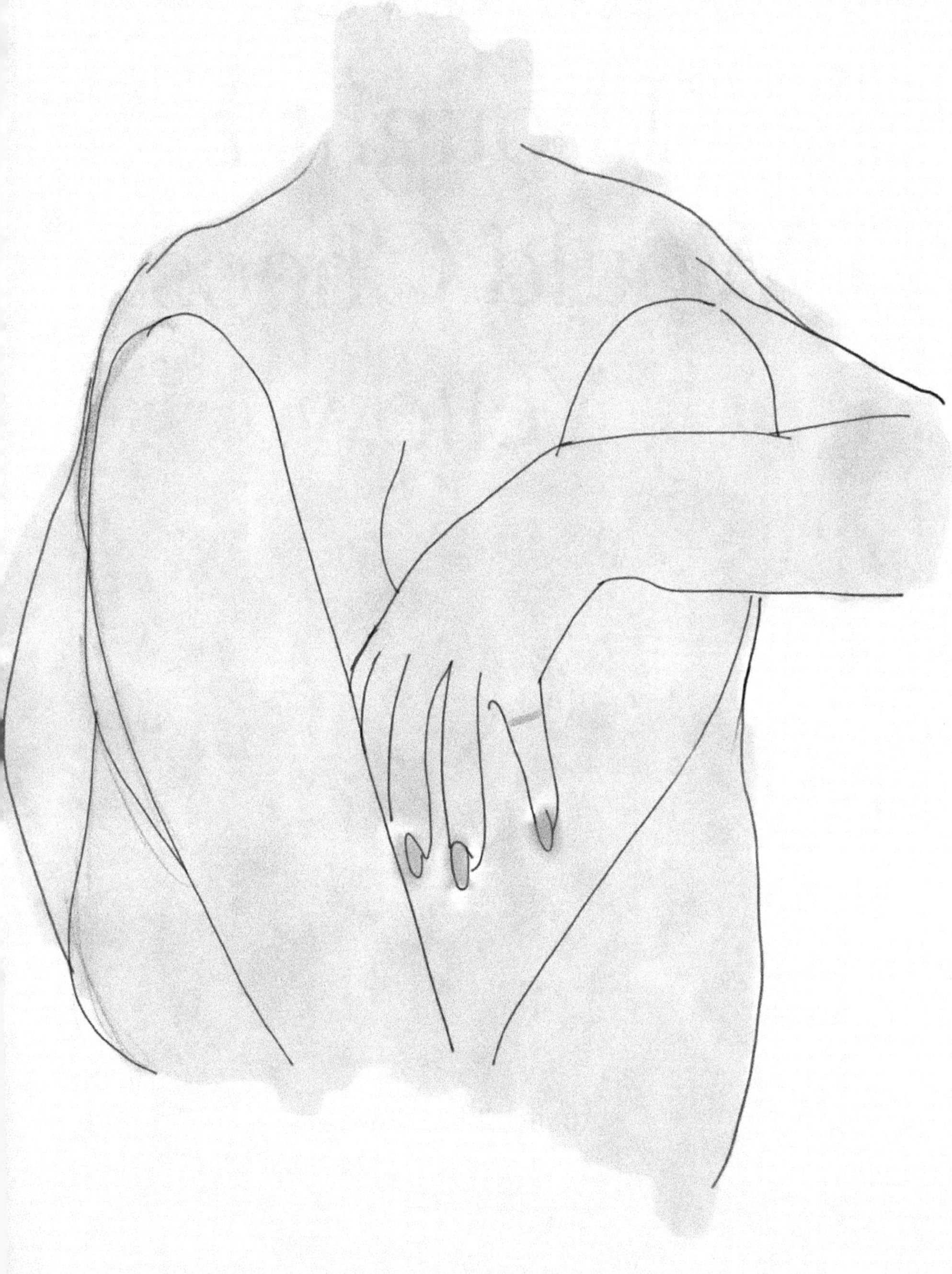

I Never Thought I Would Choose Yellow

Attallah Blake Rashad

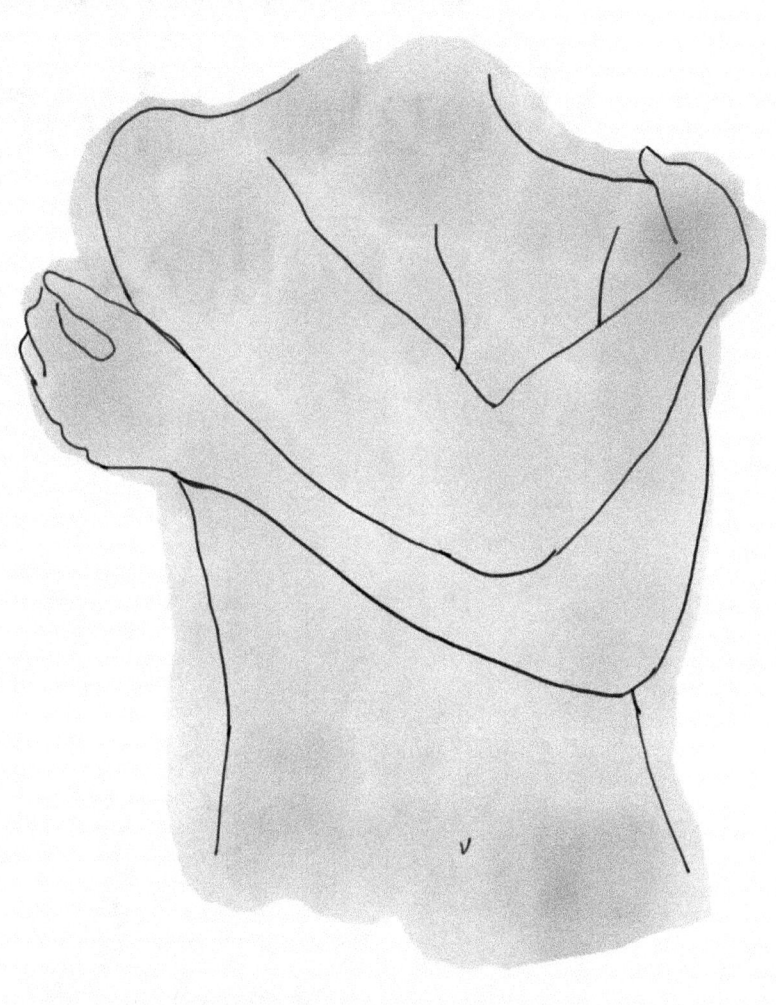

I Never Thought I Would Choose Yellow

Attallah Blake Rashad

To every race, every gender and all beings:
with love, we are one.

This book is best served in solitude with a glass of wine or tea.

Fem-i-nine
/ˈfemene/
adjective

1. *having qualities or appearance traditionally associated with women, especially delicacy and prettiness.*

A special thanks to Latif Rashad for motivating me to keep moving and join you on the journey towards success in my own way and at my own pace. You bring me clarity. Thank you to Rasheeda Slade for placing the seeds into my soil that have nourished my being. Thank you to Jeffrey Pina for telling me I could "sing."

I wouldn't have the courage to share these words without your support.

Thank you.

I Never Thought I Would Choose Yellow

Attallah Blake Rashad

Mine

i am a work of art
this much is souly true
each and every piece placed exactly right
the lines that shape my chest
the o's and the u's
these shapes, make my body mine
with the right moves
i can change those lines
make them curve, and draw in eyes
the curves that shape my lips
desire you tight in grip
the small ones that stand out best
live across my chest
lines that carve my body
make my body all mine.

One of Seven Seas

if i must describe you as anything
it would have to be the ocean
the change in current
reminds me deeply of the changes your heart make
the changes your mind create
some days you are warm to touch
and others you are so cold
you push your waters onto me
then take them back with ease
as if you never rushed in
leaving me cold from the salted sea
yet and still, i yearn your return
the give and take of your waves
keep me controlled
you speak to my body in ways
that cause my heart confusion
but the conversations between you and i
when the sun sets
bring me tranquility
i could swim your sea for eternity.

Undefined

i find myself searching the same places for you
this a desperation my heart can not define
i still wish we never ended
and you still were mine.

3 a.m.

somehow you are capable of creating toxins in my heart and passion that touches my soul.

3 a.m. II

i have always known you to not be the one i would love last but losing you is something i am forever finding hard to get past.

Virgo

i see the lights create shadows around your almond eyes
as you hide in a dark room
the hues of red and blue
you don't belong here
the scenery is too loud for a person of such solitude
let's leave together
let's go away someplace without sound
the real you speaks beautifully
when no one is around.

Virgin Ways

i remember my purity being visible
now i'm constantly trying to prove my virgin ways
it is clear i have been tainted with
i just wonder if you have ever truly noticed
and if you know me so well, why are you still here?
my soul is not clean
my heart in need of mending
somehow you have overlooked all that i'm pretending
although, you have never experienced me, in pure form
you rise peace within me
peace i thought was long gone
when you are near
i'm reminded of myself in her brightest days
you bring out my virgin ways.

A Bluebird's Heart

let's toast to being without our hearts tied
what we are fighting for, exists no more
let's break the chains of our ending love
to move on
be free of each other
a place without the horror
no more broken dishes or the slamming of the doors
the persons in the mirror we can no longer see
so please forget the things you love about me
the fighting and fucking
we don't make love anymore
don't you miss the love between our lips
now they no longer touch
darling you must see
forget the things you love about me
bluebird i want to set you free.

Dancer

even though he is dead
you are dancing with the devil everyday you keep him alive in your heart.

Raisin

the truth is
you rip me dry of emotion
and after my heart is left all dried out
somehow you convince me
to regret expressing my pain to you
even though that is the nature of my being
the reason i'm sweet.

Battle

i find myself racing against the sun
knowing time is inevitable
i stubbornly run
chasing the dreams i can not stop having
those that replay in my head a thousand times a day
over and over
the fear of letting yourself down is difficult to release
realizing it is you that control which direction you take
makes the chase a journey easier to accept.

Dreams

i've been dreaming ever since you told me yours
i can't help but wonder what this could become
where things could go
how things could be
let's talk about our unforgettable chemistry
you say it never rains when i'm with you
in my eyes we've finally escaped our rainy days
temporarily anyway
we've both got unfinished pasts
both stuck on things we thought were meant to last
those things aren't meant to be
love is a dangerous flame
and we both enjoy the fire
what we do should be forbidden
but i can not ignore the feelings given
what you bring to me
an unforgettable energy
i imagine no such bad timing
while our hearts still intertwine
see, i can dream now
ever since you told me yours.

Vacay

my lips
frozen
until i came across you
my body touched in ways i never knew
raw and thawed
just your skin close to mine
your touch sends me foreign chills within
before you i was so cold
now i have the brightest tan.

Boys Are Like Books

the words "I will **always** love you." are a lie.
this is something you say to close the book on a never
ending chapter of heartache
when you've come so far into the novel and suddenly
nothing makes sense anymore
you've reread chapters for clarity
but things just do not add up
but you don't want to give up now
because things could possibly change
perhaps the climax is near
or maybe
just maybe there's a sequel
because boys are like books.

Self

as the world revolves around me
i would be sure of myself
i could rise temperatures through your bodies with ease
i would make people feel beautiful after being touched by my grace
to spread love, happiness and laughter
i would rise each and every day
rain or snow
and give you my love the only way i know how

– Sun

3 a.m. III

note to self: stop searching for depth in those who to them, "it's not even that deep."

When The Clouds Dance

i want you to think of the two of us
as individual flowers in a field of sod
with our survival dependent on the rays of the Sun
somedays beyond our control the clouds will dance
and the Sun we desperately long for
will not be there to provide us with it's nutrients
we must learn to be deprived
be hungry
knowing the Sun will always return
with patience
we can await it's recurrence
and stand strong while the clouds dance

3a.m. VI

somehow i have managed to fall for a liar who leaves my bed at 3 a.m. and never kisses me goodbye.

Stained

i have a heart too and it is heaviest knowing you don't notice me.
this feeling has become too familiar
and my heart is beginning to sink too deep for saving
i think to myself
maybe i have forgotten it all and maybe the scars you have carved into my heart have finally healed
yet the broken glass on the mahogany still strikes my toes
how could you leave it all for me to fix?
i ask myself
where did things go wrong in your mind?
you never spoke with vulnerability
maybe i would have been forgiving
but how can i be?
knowing your love has a limit

KIN

if even you
my own kin
cannot see me and we share the same smile
the same brown eyes, the same blood
flowing through our bodies
i have a heart too but i am through chasing you.

3 a.m. V

does proving to you i love myself mean making love to someone else?

— questions i'm afraid to ask you.

Millennial Lover Part 1

we fight
between cotton and silk
we laugh
a lot
this is when it all feels there between us
yet at 3 a.m. you let go of my hand
i can feel you distancing yourself by then
years later
deeply into our affair
we lack romance
yet we live in fear
had our love become an obligation?
before my mind goes to wonder
you'd say no such accusation is fair
because our love a is privilege
only you and i share

Scorpio

feared by many
women and by men
although i am a chaser of passion and love
i can labeled as aggressive or *crazy*
the way i love you can seem defeating to others
yet it is the most unforgettable kind
many lovers find me full of strength and power
yet are still surprised by my dominance
some may even be turned off by it
it's hard to believe i mean no harm
when my exterior is frightening to see
but i can assure you i won't harm your heart
if you dare to begin to understand me.

Choose

this is coming from my deepest feelings
those that have laid a nest in my heart
i can't go on with you
but i know not how to lead my thoughts to victory
how can i begin to separate our hearts
when we've grown so close to one another
i know this feeling of weakness will turn angry
and that is quite frightening
but how do we close the door to our love
to become strangers
without ending up fighting

Millennial Lover Part 2

several seasons have passed
and between you and i
still lies confusion
between the emotional emptiness, laughter and
meaningless love we make
lies the love we have for one another
which often feels fake
i imagine you must be yearning for something more
but you never physically leave me, for long
you are always willing to take me back
and with you i admit to be willing as well.

2Faced

i would never show you this side of me
because the love you have for me will be forever changed
that i am afraid
there is an ego that lies beneath my eyes
he sings to me
controlling my thoughts
and my vision
he won't allow you near the kindness of my heart
because it belongs to him.

A Weak Without You

i am starving
my body weak from hunger pains
i am thirsty
desperately yearning the elements of earth
i am burning
i need nothing more than shade
the tips of my fingers frozen
my lips numb and cold
i am uneasy because only you nourished my soul.

Boundaries

just undress me
take off the layers on my body
that shield you
from getting too close
don't be afraid to touch me
remove the layers closer to my skin
the raw, the real and the flawed
undress me
cross the lines i have secretly drawn
if you want all of me
free me of these threads
uncover my true hue
just undress me
wash me clean of this Patchouli Absolute
reveal my purities
release my fears
just undress me
and i will take things from there.

Let Down

no one i've known
has been worthy of my heart
not even you
usually you give me the idea of love
and with that i'd like to run
far
in the same breath
taking it all away
your mind leads the downfall
how you see life
i'd like to be the judge
i can revoke my love in a split second
and make this all disappear
depending on the let down of my own thoughts
which are my fears

September

i count the time until i am near him next
i've never chased a man as far as i am willing to chase him
the savory yet sweetness of his smell
the Tom Ford, Tobacco Vanille
the brisk scent of his unwashed denim
his sweat
his untamed hair
his eyes are like honey
or the juice of an olive
good for your soul
his uncertainty delights me
i mean it excites me
i'm embarrassed to say
i enjoy his manhood forcefully locking around my lips
i like to take my time
as he smothers me in sweat and love
he controls me
he restricts my heart
but when he's asked does he *love* me
he can't tell me
i hate how he does that
and i hate that i allow it all
i prefer words
because with words i am home
and time is on my side
no need to count the time

Contra-addicting

you feel doomed at the thought of loneliness
you describe this as a fear
to be alone is not what you seek
but your feelings you don't share.

Mixed Feelings

angelic and pure
her hairs wild and thick
i find peace in your eyes
joy in kissing your lips
the words you let out and spare
the joy coming from the stories we'd share
because no matter how you spell it
she always reads me the same way
i find something comforting
in knowing you won't let me be alone
me and my mixed feelings.

February

has my heart become a burden to you?
i find myself drowning in tears
at nearly 2 a.m. on the 14th
the keyboard of my computer is unclear
i can't write your wrongs
with the water that is filling my eyes
why do i keep giving you excuses?
why do i allow mistreatment from someone who is smaller than me?
whose love does not reach my peak
i must let you go
you keep my heart sore
but these words i am too afraid to speak.

Shield

i believe love should have battles
but love should not cause you to shield your heart.

One Night Stand

you made it feel so real
jokes on me
you won't be calling me back
gave you a jewel for a stone
way before my number was even saved in your phone
funny thing is, i knew
you were nothing special
or packing it either
ignored my intuition
even with all reason
treated my body like it didn't mean much
i have shared it with a couple, maybe even a few
do i cross your mind?
i backspace each text
reread
rewrite
then release.

Running

i have been trying to escape you for so long
why won't my heart let me leave you?

Searching

i have written many love letters
those past lovers would have surely kept
yet i'm still not finished writing one to myself.

The Wait

i've waited for you so long
now that you are here
having you close
isn't something i crave
it is something i fear

Ego

slow down
stop pretending to care
stop saying you love me
you need me
because those are the things i want to hear.

Undo

each thought unfolds and becomes you
each feeling i numb away
you kiss me
only when the lights are low
you love me
in your own way
it is that kind of love i don't desire
love me the way i tell you i need to be loved
because only then
you will fuel my fire

Record I

some nights i find myself wondering
what life would be like without you
i begin to fantasize being without you
i seem happier
as much as i am afraid to actually take the pill
i'd rather just envision the potential
i wonder what it is like to not wonder if i'm enough
but to know
you never seem satisfied
even when i'm doing more than i feel i should
it is still never quite enough

Record II

everyday it gets harder
i don't know how to describe it
but it is icy and it is deep
a chill through my chest
i notice so many things about you
i wish to ignore
i can't
not forever
eventually i will have to undress them
but for now i feel empty
unloved
unwanted
and i allow it
you turn it off and on
somehow
how do you?
when you turn it on, it is so genuine
when you turn it off, it is so cold
there is just no in between

The Thinker

it's hard to love a man of logic
because when i go in to kiss your lips
you'd overthink how you'd prefer our lips to meet
when i'm with you
i rarely think of what could go wrong
i'm too busy chasing the feeling
don't use your logic to love me for too long
don't love me carefully
love me care-freely

No Woman

a woman of my fruit
her love shall not have bounds
she should never ask for love
nor affection
how does a woman of such quality
dare ask to be touched
asked to be understood
even asked to be loved
no woman of my fruit
shall ever taste a second handed love

Sleeping Alone in Love

my bed sheets are cold
and warm just before midnight
as our lips lock throughout the night
passion drives through our bodies
and my sheets turn cold again as i lay there alone
just before 3 a.m.
you check your phone
i watch you leave
when will i get tired of waiting around for you to love me
like i deserve to be?

A Mother of 9

to a mother of nine
who could not find the time to love me
to a mother who could put a man above me
to a woman, torn
her womb to which i was born
i find it difficult to forgive you
i try not to point fingers
or call you by another name
because you are *my mother*
i wish you would have taken the time to love me
the way you loved the ones who brought us pain.

a Break

as i poison my body
for a temporary emotional fix
i find at night
it is you i truly miss
no mind is paid to the guy in between my thighs
because he is just not you.
my eyes drown in tears made of salt
i suffer most in the morning
when i realize what i hoped was a dream
was reality
i am surrounded by strangers
my mind filled with fluids of confusion
every moment we don't share
it is us we are losing.

Drawn In

many lovers don't last between my thighs.
this they will admit.
many lovers are drawn in by the darkness in my eyes.
with this they will submit.

May

we met in darkness
with the touch of your hand
you brought me to sanity
your kind of escape
new to me

just a few weeks together
before your love lifted me high
you instilled love and life into me
effortlessly that summer before July.

By Summer

i knew long ago that my love for you grew strong
i never showed you what my heart felt
i apologize
my lips did not share the truth
i was afraid to leave the darkness
and hold onto your hand.

Sunset Blvd

as the layers of orange temporarily mask the sky
my heart begins to reject at the seam.
the seam, that kept our hearts intertwined
memories reminiscent at the sight of your face
soon disappear as my mind begins to race.

Game

my heart breaks every time i play this game
it's something like losing the use of my heart
and somehow still breathing, standing and still awaiting
the next contender.

Like Honey

i find comfort looking into your honey colored eyes
comfort i once could not find in another lover's arms.

Follow

show me the way
you asked
show me the way to your heart
you said
show me how to love you
you begged
but you'll let me down
i said

Caught Up

i counted down the days until i would see you again
only because to be with you was forbidden
we never had much time together
our romance
like ice
melting with every kiss

Why?

why do i love you?
who does not wish to speak
your love is shallow.
your love is not memorable.
your love does not penetrate me.

Candy

the heartbreak is more promising than the falling in love
inevitably the future of love is a broken heart
while the future of heartbreak is happiness.

Closed

passion.
romance.
depth.
steam.
is what his love lacks

Prisoner

how much longer must she imprison herself
this lack of love is eating away at her passion filled heart
free her heart
free her body
free her soul

Temptation

my body depends on you deeply
as i await your presence to warm me up
i can see the death of him and i more clearly
every moment with you
between linen and silk
i desire and lust after
there is only so much i can take before i spill out
and completely lose sight of him
as i am too busy chasing you.

October 28th

she is passion.
she has been filled with darkness.
drowned by light.
she is passion.
her body driven by the waters of her nature.
lust fills her eyes in the form of man and material.
she takes pride in who she is
knowing she can't be tamed
miss october twenty-eighth.

Wyd?

you are all i think about
you make it hard for me
when you call
to just talk
or come by
to just see me
what are you doing?

Excuses

is this what you planned for your heart
tell me the fucking truth
tell me that you made a mistake
tell me you don't feel good about us anymore
tell me you are not happy
so i can give myself an excuse to run away

Message to:

i'm losing all control
and it's getting dark outside
come inside, my love
and stay here
i'm falling in love.

Powerful Women

i can start fires
fires in the souls
of the men that cross my path
those that try to dim the light in my eyes
so that i can see *them*.

F* Boy

he tells me i'm not good enough because
he loves me half way
he loves me half way
because he's not good enough.

Money

he tries to control me
by touching me slowly
and leaving me quickly.

Nude

i realize
i can not be tamed
and i will not be controlled
by a replaceable penis
with a stroke that does not fulfill me

24

i get tired of you too easily
lying that i am still interested
when i don't know for sure what interests me at all
at twenty four.

Hunger

i want to be touched more
frequently
but with you this has become impossible
with a soul like mine
how can i deserve to be deprived
of what i give so purely

Meditation

inhale love.
even when exhausted
inhale love.

Combination

i feel at peace in your darkness
don't unlock the door
keep me safe

Mirror

i don't feel beautiful today
i'm not sure if it is lack of sleep
or lack of love
or maybe it is because
i didn't wear any earrings today.

Days

you have never said "i love you."
and it has been over a thousand days
i tell myself our love is different
but is it love at all?

Fans

the people who told me i can't
are in the audience right now
searching for imperfections
well there is plenty to go around

Love is to Death

if you want to know what death feels like
love deeply
then hurt the one you love
the one you would have loved
the longest.

Rainbow

i'm growing
my colors are changing
i'm going
i'm gone
and now it's raining.

Darkness

if i don't keep running
i'll never escape this darkness
i'll never escape my pain.

Unison

if we are one
why am i always alone?

Dreams

i believe your dreams tell you how you feel
well i dreamt you died
when i awoke i searched for your existence.

Allure

i find you so alluring
while the sun is at it's peak
i love you
but at this very moment
i choose not to speak.

Soon

i dream of maple finished floors
and making you breakfast in silk.
kissing you in the mornings
while you hold me.
your hands on the curve of my back
or the tip of my hips.

Fireplaces

i watch as material things excite you
but i can only offer my heart
which does not ignite you.

Tell Me

i wonder when the time stops
then will you realize?
when the time stops
will you then know?
when it is all too late
then will you let your love show?

Storm

let my love cause a flood in your mind
heavy waves in your heart
let my storm wash you away

Rejection

even though i don't want anyone near
i would invite you anyway
make you fall for me
my love would affect you similar to a dream
knowing that would be untrue
i'd just reject you

Midnight

some nights a sad song seemed so satisfying
then there were others when i was crying
swimming an endless sea of heartache
replaying our memories
those good and those bad
i miss you at midnight
i miss what we had.

Truthful Lies

i always wanted to tell you how i felt
but i knew you would run
not literally but emotionally
and that would be the last time we'd speak
so i'll tell you a truthful lie
just to keep you by my side.

"We're Just Friends."

do you knowingly hold me hostage? or are you as simple as you seem?

Unsexy

i appreciate the negative energies because they fuel my creative power. tell me i'm not sexy. tell me i amount to nothing. tell me you don't love me.

Heartache

time has gifted us closure
yet i still reminisce the purity and youth of our love
i still think of you as a true love
you touched me so deeply
so deeply
i know your intention still lives
but in my heart
you have died.

Help Me Forget

my heart rejected it's home
when i heard your voice.
i didn't look for you once
but i thought of you the whole night.

Whiskey

i get faded when i don't hear from you
i get drunk when you don't call.
is it this easy for you to avoid me
don't you love me at all?

Mistakenly

look what i have gotten myself into
this twisted love
was just a fantasy
now you are making plans with me.

Songs

i find it difficult to write love songs
because i have never experienced love
not in the flesh
not in the mind
not until the very moment we met
the things i can't forget

2 Late

the day i confess my love to you will be the day it dies while we let fear control our hearts.

1st Love

just because i loved you for long
doesn't mean we should continue
i'm growing
i'm changing
you and i were high school
i mean i'm a rose now
i'm a rainbow
and i have out grown your garden.

Like Summer

it feels like summer when you hold onto my hips
i feel it's summer when we kiss
our bodies become one
i love when we touch like this.

Sincerely, Your Daughter

i wish i knew what it was like to feel your love again
instead i search for it in others
i desperately want you to love me
accept me
i miss you
i miss hearing your voice
when other girls talk about you
their mother
my soul
it burns
it's like fire
it's like rage
then it's hatred
it's jealously
and it's pain
then the water runs endlessly
i want your love again.

♥

i realize i can't love you
for some reason my heart won't allow it
i'm wasting your time
i'm afraid
i'm trying
and i don't feel anything.

Forrest Lane

my roots are deep
my hair is wild
the trees growing rapidly
new flowers
are blooming
find your purpose before they tear us down.

Love is to Fear

we talk all day
yet i have much more to say
words i'm so afraid to communicate
with just the thought of you not wanting to stay

Reverse

i think of you from time to time
wondering if i could hear your voice
just once more
would that change how i feel
at this very moment
while i am most afraid of the future
would the sound of your words
bring me clarity
would i want you back around?

Room 13

how did you become my dark shadow
with me when i'm asleep
there when i awake

Scars

i have scars drawn onto my heart
deeply
scars on my body
that are visible
to only you
i'm dying inside
please don't love me
while my time here is running out

Finally...

i feel you deeply now
finally, after so long
when we kiss
i feel forever
when we make love
we sweat
we bond together
i feel you deeply now

They

i've been loving you
in darkness
when no one is watching
we kiss
we laugh
we touch
now that they watch our every move
i can't do this with you
i don't love you anymore

Sunday Morning

i watch you as you sleep
dreaming
i slip out of bed in silence
slicing fruit
toasting bread
scrambling eggs
i feel the need to feed you
my fruit belongs to you
i belong to you
sunday

Good Morning

as i set to start the day
i see my reflection in the objects
that mirror my features
my eyes
my nose
my lips
i am a powerful
woman
i am a lover
a lover
i am at peace with my being

1992

your body never forgets the trauma it experienced
even if the mind tells it to.

Ex

i watched you cheer on our mutual friend
i sipped champagne
you caused a scene
twice
you slept with my friends
you threw dirt on my name
as i left the party
i heard you call out my name
"i love you."
but you bring me great pain.

Jeffrey

my first and only love
my longest lover
do you feel it too?
the years to come
the moments to share
knowing you will always be there
brings me comfort
and fear
it's in between
i'll never forget you

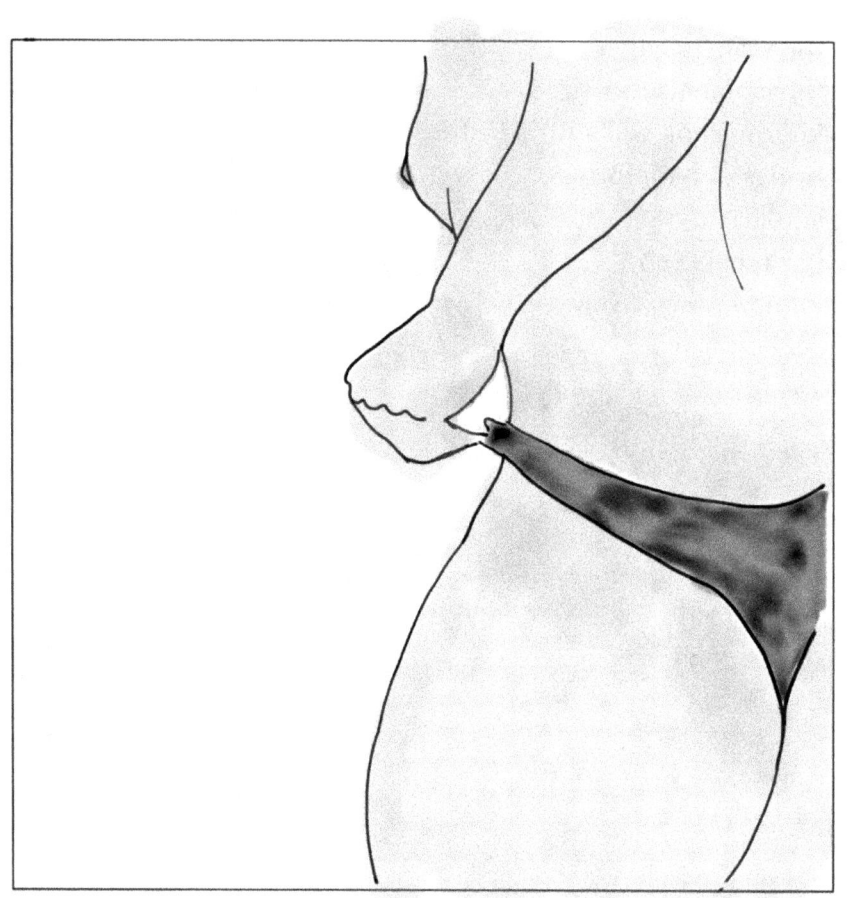

Thank you.